FLOWER·FAIRIES OF·THE·TREES

Designed by Malcolm Smythe

Colour retouched by Elsa Godfrey

Copyright © 1985 The Estate of Cicely Mary Barker

This edition first published in hardback 1985,
and in paperback 1987 by
Blackie and Son Limited
7 Leicester Place, London WC2H 7BP

British Library Cataloguing in Publication Data
Barker, Cicely Mary
     Flower fairies of the trees.———(The flower fairies)
     I. Title   II. Series
     821'.912   PR6003.A6786
     ISBN 0-216-91717-4
     ISBN 0-216-92154-6 Pbk

Printed in Great Britain by Cambus Litho, East Kilbride

FLOWER·FAIRIES OF·THE·TREES

Poems and pictures by
CICELY MARY BARKER

BLACKIE

THE SONG OF THE
POPLAR FAIRY

White fluff is drifting like snow round our feet;
  Puff! it goes blowing
  Away down the street.

Where does it come from? Look up and see!
  There, from the Poplar!
  Yes, from that tree!

Tassels of silky white fluffiness there
  Hang among leaves
  All a-shake in the air.

Fairies, you well may guess, use it to stuff
  Pillows and cushions,
  And play with it – puff!

POPLAR

THE SONG OF THE
SILVER BIRCH
FAIRY

There's a gentle tree with a satiny bark,
All silver-white, and upon it, dark,
Is many a crosswise line and mark –
  She's a tree there's no mistaking!
The Birch is this light and lovely tree,
And as light and lovely still is she
When the Summer's time has come to flee,
  As she was at Spring's awakening.

She has new Birch-catkins, small and tight,
Though the old ones scatter
 and take their flight,
And the little leaves, all yellow and bright,
  In the autumn winds are shaking.
And with fluttering wings
 and hands that cling,
The fairies play and the fairies swing
On the fine thin twigs,
 that will toss and spring
  With never a fear of breaking.

SILVER BIRCH

THE SONG OF THE
CHERRY TREE
FAIRY

Cherries, a treat for the blackbirds;
    Cherries for girls and boys;
And there's never an elf in the treetops
    But cherries are what he enjoys!

Cherries in garden and orchard,
    Ripe and red in the sun;
And the merriest elf in the treetops
    Is the fortunate Cherry-tree one!

CHERRY TREE

THE SONG OF THE
WILLOW FAIRY

By the peaceful stream or the shady pool
I dip my leaves in the water cool.

Over the water I lean all day,
Where the sticklebacks and the minnows play.

I dance, I dance, when the breezes blow,
And dip my toes in the stream below.

WILLOW

THE SONG OF THE
PEAR BLOSSOM
FAIRY

Sing, sing, sing, you blackbirds!
　　Sing, you beautiful thrush!
It's Spring, Spring, Spring; so sing, sing, sing,
　　From dawn till the stars say "hush".

See, see, see the blossom
　　On the Pear Tree shining white!
It will fall like snow, but the pears will grow
　　For people's and birds' delight.

Build, build, build, you chaffinch;
　　Build, you robin and wren,
A safe warm nest where your eggs may rest;
　　Then sit, sit, sit, little hen!

PEAR BLOSSOM

THE SONG OF THE
LILAC FAIRY

White May is flowering,
　　Red May beside;
Laburnum is showering
　　Gold far and wide;
But *I* sing of Lilac,
　　The dearly loved Lilac,
Lilac, in Maytime
　　A joy and a pride!

I love her so much
　　That I never can tell
If she's sweeter to look at,
　　Or sweeter to smell.

LILAC

THE SONG OF THE
SWEET CHESTNUT
FAIRY

Chestnuts, sweet Chestnuts,
   To pick up and eat,
Or keep until Winter,
   When, hot, they're a treat!

Like hedgehogs, their shells
   Are prickly outside;
But silky within,
   Where the little nuts hide,

Till the shell is split open,
   And, shiny and fat,
The Chestnut appears;
   Says the Fairy: "How's *that*?"

SWEET CHESTNUT

THE SONG OF THE
WILD CHERRY BLOSSOM FAIRY

In April when the woodland ways
    Are all made glad and sweet
With primroses and violets
    New-opened at your feet,
       Look up and see
        A fairy tree,
       With blossoms white
       In clusters light,
All set on stalks so slender,
    With pinky leaves so tender.
O Cherry tree, wild Cherry tree!
    You lovely, lovely thing to see!

WILD CHERRY BLOSSOM

THE SONG OF THE
SYCAMORE FAIRY

Because my seeds have wings, you know,
    They fly away to earth;
And where they fall, why, there they grow –
    New Sycamores have birth!
Perhaps a score? Oh, hundreds more!
    Too many, people say!
And yet to me it's fun to see
    My winged seeds fly away.
(But first they must turn ripe and brown,
    And lose their flush of red;
And *then* they'll all go twirling down
    To earth, to find a bed.)

SYCAMORE

THE SONG OF THE
ALMOND BLOSSOM
FAIRY

Joy! the Winter's nearly gone!
Soon will Spring come dancing on;
And, before her, here dance I,
Pink like sunrise in the sky.
Other lovely things will follow;
Soon will cuckoo come, and swallow;
Birds will sing and buds will burst,
But the Almond is the first!

ALMOND BLOSSOM

THE SONG OF THE
ELM TREE FAIRY

Soft and brown in Winter-time,
Dark and green in Summer's prime,
All their leaves a yellow haze
In the pleasant Autumn days –
See the lines of Elm trees stand
Keeping watch through all the land
Over lanes, and crops, and cows,
And the fields where Dobbin ploughs.
All day long, with listening ears,
Sits the Elm-tree Elf, and hears
Distant bell, and bleat, and bark,
Whistling boy, and singing lark.
Often on the topmost boughs
Many a rook has built a house;
Evening comes; and overhead,
Cawing, home they fly to bed.

ELM TREE

THE SONG OF THE
ASH TREE FAIRY

Trunk and branches are smooth and grey;
      Ash-grey, my honey!
The buds of the Ash-tree, black are they;
      And the days are long and sunny.

The leaves make patterns against the sky,
      Blue sky, my honey!
And the keys in bunches hang on high;
      To call them "keys" is funny!

Each with its seed, the keys hang there,
      Still there, my honey!
When the leaves are gone
  and the woods are bare;
      Short days may yet be sunny.

ASH TREE

THE SONG OF THE
LABURNUM FAIRY

All Laburnum's
Yellow flowers
Hanging thick
In happy showers –
Look at them!
The reason's plain
Why folks call them
"Golden Rain"!
"Golden Chains"
They call them too,
Swinging there
Against the blue.

LABURNUM

THE SONG OF THE
ALDER FAIRY

By the lake or river-side
   Where the Alders dwell,
In the Autumn may be spied
Baby catkins; cones beside –
   Old and new as well.
Seasons come and seasons go;
   That's the tale they tell!

After Autumn, Winter's cold
   Leads us to the Spring;
And, before the leaves unfold,
On the Alder you'll behold,
   Crimson catkins swing!
They are making ready now:
   That's the song I sing!

ALDER

THE SONG OF THE
BEECH TREE
FAIRY

The trunks of Beeches are smooth and grey,
    Like tall straight pillars of stone
In great Cathedrals where people pray;
    Yet from tiny things they've grown.
About their roots is the moss; and wide
    Their branches spread, and high;
It seems to us, on the earth who bide,
    That their heads are in the sky.

And when Spring is here,
    and their leaves appear,
    With a silky fringe on each,
Nothing is seen so new and green
    As the new young green of Beech.
O the great grey Beech is young, is young,
    When, dangling soft and small,
Round balls of bloom from its twigs are hung
    And the sun shines over all.

BEECH TREE

THE SONG OF THE
ELDER FAIRY

When the days have grown in length,
When the sun has greater power,
Shining in his noonday strength;
When the Elder Tree's in flower;
When each shady kind of place
By the stream and up the lane
Shows its mass of creamy lace –
Summer's really come again!

ELDER

THE SONG OF THE
MULBERRY FAIRY

"Here we go round the Mulberry bush!"
   You remember the rhyme – oh yes!
      But which of you know
      How mulberries grow
   On the slender branches, drooping low?
      Not many of you, I guess.

Someone goes round the Mulberry bush
   When nobody's there to see;
      He takes the best
      And leaves the rest,
   From top to toe like a Mulberry drest:
      This fat little fairy's he!

MULBERRY

THE SONG OF THE
LIME TREE
FAIRY

Bees! bees! come to the trees
Where the Lime has hung her treasures;
　　Come, come, hover and hum;
　　Come and enjoy your pleasures!
The feast is ready, the guests are bidden;
　　Under the petals the honey is hidden;
Like pearls shine the drops of sweetness there,
And the scent of the Lime-flowers fills the air,
But soon these blossoms pretty and pale
Will all be gone; and the leaf-like sail
Will bear the little round fruits away;
　　So bees! bees! come while you may!

LIME TREE

THE SONG OF THE
GUELDER ROSE
FAIRIES

There are two little trees:
In the garden there grows
The one with the snowballs;
All children love *those*!

The other small tree
Not everyone knows,
With her blossoms spread flat –
Yet they're both Guelder Rose!

But the garden Guelder has nothing
    When her beautiful balls are shed;
While in Autumn her wild little sister
    Bears berries of ruby red!

GUELDER ROSE